"Mary Walker isn't just one of my favorite living poets. She's one of my favorite poets, period. She has an astonishing gift for making a few precise words and images sink deep into the mind and heart, bringing chills of recognition, flashes of joy, rivers of comfort. I'll keep this book close and read it often. I advise other readers to do the same!" ~ *Martha Beck, New York Times bestselling author*

"I am on poem number four, and I have decided this book is going to change my year." ~ *Amber-Jayne Bain, Photographer*

"If you love Mary Oliver and David Whyte, you will love Mary Walker. If you love the earth, you will love Mary Walker. She is a poet of nature and the soul. The Land Will Hold You nourishes body, mind, and spirit." ~ *Melanie Phoenix, Poet & Writer*

"To all the poetry lovers out there, this book is an absolute treasure." ~ *Wellington Apothecary*

"The poems are so poignant and considered. I love their precision, insights and the way they prompt powerful visual experiences, particularly for me since I spend so much time on the land studying it." ~ *Deborah Moss, Artist.*

"Your book has arrived and it is absolutely beautiful. My body breathes a soft sigh of relief everytime I read one." ~ *Joss Goulden, Aware Parenting instructor*

"These poems are like medicine." ~ *Chantal Cropp, Ethnobotanist & Writer*

"A tonic for the part of my soul that remembers what it's like to love, and be loved by, a landscape that's thrillingly alive and infinitely loving." ~ *Emma Campbell Webster, Poet, Writer & Performer*

"Mine is by my bedside where I dip in for my last waking thought before turning out the light." ~ *Sarah Hatcher, Artist.*

"This already feels like a much-treasured book." ~ *Katrina Rowe*

"My book arrived a couple of weeks ago. I have been savoring every poem. This is one I will gift to many friends." ~ *Deanna de Paoli*

Published in New Zealand by
Castle Press
PO Box 47165
Upper Hutt 5143
New Zealand

A catalogue record is available at the National Library of New Zealand.

ISBN: 978-0-473-72519-8 (hardback)
ISBN: 978-0-473-72518-1 (paperback)
ISBN: 978-0-473-72520-4 (epub)

Cover design: Sara Gaspar
Printed by Ingram Spark

CASTLE
PRESS

home

poems for becoming who you are
and releasing who you're not

Mary Walker

ALSO BY MARY WALKER

Lullaby for Mothers: motherhood in poems

The Land Will Hold You

This book is dedicated to Marion Rose

CONTENTS

Introduction   11

Come Home   15
Sometimes, Go Back   16
Thaw   17
Soften   18
Relief   19
Seeds   20
Mend   21
Alone   22
The Return   23
From Dust   24
Clear   25
Look   26
Rupture   27
Listen   28
Unhitch   29
Incremental   30
Homecoming   31
Excavate   32
Grace   33
Wings   34
Choice   35
The Match   36
Encircle   37
Steady   38
Lighthouse   39
Even   40

Fire 41

Navigating 42

Many Paths 43

At Hand 44

Here Now 45

On Asking 46

Quiet 47

The Still Pond 48

When You Know 49

Replenish 50

Freed 51

The Invitation 52

Keep Something For Yourself 53

Wait 54

Be Not Silent 55

Another Way 56

Change 57

Clay 58

Terrain 59

Mind 60

Joy 61

Unafraid 62

Awaken 63

Esteem 64

Right Action 65

The Line 66

When Life Brings You to an Edge 67

As It Is 68

This Way, Come 69

Rest 70

Keep Going   71
Rearrange   72
Pennies   73
While You Can   74
Woven   75
Loose   76
Homeward   77
Pieces   78
Imminent   79
The Stream   80
Resolution   81
New   82
Trust the Tide   83
The Path   84
Vessel   85
Ever Learning   86
Beyond the Map   87
What I Want From Life   88
Re-Entry   89
It's Not Too Late   90
Home   92

Index of First Lines   94
Acknowledgements   97

INTRODUCTION

Though time seems to unroll along a straight line, life rarely does. Our past is often still with us, inviting or demanding we look back. It's less like a straight line, and more like a spiral. We notice recurring themes in our lives. We hurt in unique and particular ways, and these hurts become familiar. We feel like we are looping around, passing the same landmark time and again. Or worse, going backwards. Equally, there are times when our life leaps forward. Passions are revealed, gifts unfold, opportunities arise. Life contains it all, the enjoyable and the painful.

Home supports you on this journey. The poems coalesced around the idea of coming closer to ourselves, and of finding our true home. As the collection came together I was reminded of the grass labyrinth we created in 2019. Unlike a maze, a labyrinth has only one path. It leads you to the centre and out again. And although it looks like a spiral taking you ever closer, the path actually doubles back on itself constantly. One moment you think you're almost there, a few steps later you are back at the outer edge. If you don't understand the labyrinth's design, it can be infuriating. A bit like life. From a distance we have perspective on what's happening and can see the patterns playing out. But as in a labyrinth, when we are deep in it, all we can do is trust where we are and trust the path.

These poems were written as I navigated the ups and downs of my own life. They represent the wide range of experience as we heal the past and become more of who we are. Some poems meet us in our sadness, some remind us to embrace joy. Some offer solace, while some encourage or even present a fiery call to arms. Some poems are about releasing the past, and some invite us to embrace the present moment. Just as life contains up and downs, so the poems in this book weave back and forth between releasing and becoming.

The labyrinth was one source of support on my journey. Another vital one was the work of Marion Rose, Ph.D. It is thanks to her that I came to understand and experience the process of healing. A number of these poems were written while I was being mentored by Marion. Learning from her and receiving her support re-oriented my life. I love that through those poems you will also encounter her wisdom.

If you are on a healing journey, I invite you to take time to be with memories that arise. Don't push them away. Make room for tears. Learn how the body helps us heal, and how our hearts recover. Seek out people who can listen compassionately. Work with a counsellor, therapist or mentor if that is available to you. Most importantly, give yourself lots of compassion, spend time in nature, and rest. Whether you are tending to the past or stepping toward what calls you, remember your constant centre. Remember, always, you are home.

Come Home

Come home
though you don't know you're gone.

Come home
from you don't know where.

Come home
from all you've outgrown.

Come home
though you're tired.

Come home
though you're scared.

Come home
though you don't know the way.

Come home
from the hurts you carry.

Come home
from your lonely past.

Come home
to find yourself waiting.

Come home.

Sometimes, Go Back

Sometimes we have to go back to go forward.
Sometimes the answers to what lie ahead
are behind us.

We forgot to bring everything with us.
We mistakenly brought too much.
What did you lay down like a crayon
in the middle of drawing your life?
And what did you pick up that was not yours?

What have you been carrying for somebody else?
Whose burden do you bear,
whose actions did you claim
as, somehow, your own fault?

Sometimes the answers are behind us.
Sometimes we have to go back
to collect who we are
and return who we're not.
Sometimes we have to go back to go forward.

Thaw

After the freeze comes the thaw
and though the warning signs were plenty—
ice groaning deep in the belly,
cracks that showed on the surface,
the feel of things beginning to slip—
despite that, the speed of it,
everything freed up
slicing and skidding
and shifting,
that speed, after standing still for so long
takes the breath away.
This is natural, not disaster.
Move to higher ground,
watch the ice floes make their way downstream,
what was frozen getting ever smaller.
From above it's only a change of state,
only water, running free.

Soften

We want the dam to break,
we do, but the thing
is so hard packed,
jammed tight
with years of heartbreak,
frustration, sadness
and loss.
We are a river of tears,
frozen in place,
stratified, fossilised
feeling. Where to begin?

A little weep
to start things off,
to soften the clay,
make way for our heart
dissolving.
Encourage the melt,
welcome the tears,
watch the soil in you
give way.

Relief

In the end
the moment of change
is imperceptible.
Less the arrival of light,
more a lessening of the dark—
the hand that stops the closing door,
a curtain left open an inch,
a small draught that lets the flame
fan, catch and kindle.
The smallest of windows
can lever a life wide open.

Seeds

Don't fear the fall-out
as the old ways
go by the wayside.

When has a seed
fallen from a flower
that is not fully open?

And when has that seed
grown without resting
first in the dark?

Mend

You may come loose
from the fabric of your life,
your fingers too sore
and eyes too tired
to find the way back in.

Before mother was born
you lay silent inside her,
both of you held
in grandmother's womb,
and long before that
great great grandmother
carried your grandmother too.

Grandmother knows,
so part of you knows,
how to find the dropped stitch.
Loose is not lost,
dropped is not fallen,
hanging means still connected.

Alone

When you wake into
the great loneliness,
the cold cell of disconnect,
don't turn away, don't rush
into the arms of day
begging distance and distraction
carry you home.

Alone is a mistake made early
but not one we're doomed
to wake into each day.
Missing something
simply reminds us
there is something to miss.

To wake cold and scared
is to want it back, is to know
distance and distraction
have led you from home.
Walk back to where you left yourself,
come in from the cold.

The Return

It's not that I want to improve anything,
nor change what is or is not
but to return to the empty vessel
into which I was poured,
to return to empty completeness,
that cavernous full,
the vessel, the pourer, the all.

From Dust

If you find yourself
rattling the cage of your life,
grabbing the bars
and calling for freedom,
make your way to the floor,
close your eyes
and free yourself
from all you see around you.
Here in the dark
there are no barriers,
no wardens, no cage.
It all returns to dust,
anything can be built.

Clear

How many lenses we look through,
layers of self and others
obscuring what is before us.
It is time now
to return viewpoints,
seek own counsel,
retrain the eye to see what it sees,
the heart to follow, and the mind
to release its tight-fisted grip.

Any creature that meets suffering does it,
makes clear rules to ensure a pain-free life,
though most of what we fear
has already happened,
though what we stand to lose
is living itself.
It is time now to discover
what we truly see, who we really are,
what the world and life looks like
unobstructed.

Look

The events of our life
will sometimes channel our attention,
forcing our gaze toward the otherwise unseen,
clouding the unnecessary,
cutting the extraneous,
pressing the point
upon us,
look
here.

Rupture

Heal me then, but gently.
A seed pod quietly opening.
A tree retiring its leaves.
A rose releasing petals after bloom.
Rain to end a drought.
Dawn to end the dark.
Rupture and resolution in one.

Listen

Don't placate the parts of you
that want to scream and cry,
they don't need to be filed down,
these sharp points
on which our life catches,
showing us what hurts,
showing us what's stuck,
showing us why we need
to scream and cry.
So, scream and cry.

Unhitch

Unhitch yourself from the wagon
that goes only one way,
travels only one route,
rides the same rutted path it always has,
the end of which is always known.

If it's change you're after,
if you long to feel the earth,
hear the sounds of the living,
witness lives unfolding
in real time, in time
with the living of your own

unhitch yourself from the wagon
that goes only one way,
travels only one route,
one speed, with one end in mind,
never minding where else
you might want to go.

To know what lies the other way,
how far your legs can carry you,
what the air feels like
when you're not rushing through it,
unhitch yourself from the wagon.

Incremental

This is it.
There is no epiphany coming.
No single moment,
no anointment,
no striking clarity
where the veil parts
and the curtain is torn from the wall at last.

No, the shutter opens by degrees,
the thin film peels away
one quarter inch at a time
as it has been doing,
as you have been doing
even as you swear you cannot,
even as you keep your eyes
fixed firmly on the floor.

Homecoming

After a long time unmoored,
living alongside rather than
in your self,
on seeing this
and feeling suddenly homesick
for something you didn't know existed—

peace

—you might long to rush at yourself,
to dive headlong into the safety of home
and wonder why you keep missing,
wonder why you and your life
keep floating away
from each other.

Knowing the anchor
was thrown too far from the boat
all that time ago,
reunion can't come soon enough.
Still, it takes time to reacquaint,
time to trust the tide
that was always working to take you home,
that will pick you up
and return you yet.

Excavate

Clear the rubble, sweep the soil,
with staff in hand
strike the ground

Pour forth, fury! Come, outrage!

lay hidden no longer
lest you poison the soil.

Grace

Grace comes
the way a whale comes,
nowhere to be seen then suddenly
lifting you clear of the water.

Though you called her,
you, in the boat of your life
now feel afraid, or at least dwarfed
by the weight of grace bestowed.

Immense she may be
but grace is ever gentle,
lowering you into your life again,
waiting below the skin of the sea.

Wings

The seagulls are circling
calling, as if crying
let me out.
Can't they smell the salt air?
Can't they feel the way home?
Don't we know we have wings
and open air in which to stretch them?

Choice

Each day splits
into two, again and again—
hope or despair
faith or fear
love or judgement.
Nothing is inevitable
except, at each fork in the road,
the chance to choose
and then the need
to set your foot upon it.
What would hope do?
What, faith?
What, love?

The Match

When the fire won't catch,
when the match, struck
over and over fails to take
and you find yourself
cold and alone
in the dark,
what lights easily for you?
Where do you find warmth?
When the task ahead is leaden
or not ready to be met
know the spark is still inside.
And look, the sky is lightening
all around you.

Encircle

Curl yourself around it,
no matter how strange it may seem
or what you are drawn to,
circle it with your body
a spiral with it at your centre,
absorb it through your skin
and let every cell drink in
what has been calling you.
Become it. Let it become you.

Steady

It's not others that threaten your flame
but your own ceaseless moving.

Hold steady long enough
for your flickering light to settle.

Are you pouring everything into staying alive?
Trust life has you and spend it all on burning brighter.

Lighthouse

That something
you feel called to,
the almost-voice you hear,
the thing to be done
you cannot name,
known, but now forgotten?

It's smaller than you think, that thing,
simpler than you'd dare believe,
less, but altogether more
than you imagine.

Go home and do
what brings you life.
The something you search for
is no more than this,
and will make of you
a lighthouse.

Even

The flame of a candle
always licks upward,
water in a glass
stays level with the earth
however unsteady the hand.
There are forces mightier than you,
hands that hold you here
until your water lies eternally still,
your flame rises finally up,
and still you'll be held, even.

Fire

Cradled in your palm
you have kept the flame alive,
kept it from the elements,
fed it enough to stay alight
but not so much as to
burn the hold that holds it.
You have watched and waited for the place
in which you could finally set it down,
finally set the flame free
and watch the smoke rise.
Listen now for the coming
of those it calls.

Navigating

Frightening thoughts
are roads of no return
taking you places
you don't want to go.
The further down that road you go
the worse you imagine things to be.
There's enough
that's intolerable in the world
without dreaming up more.
Redirect the mind.
Where?
The sun, the stars,
the moon and tides—
each proffers a steady hand,
each offers a truth
you can steer by.

Many Paths

When you find freedom
which you will,
and want to share it
which you shall,
is it freedom you will speak of
or the path you took to get there?

There are no fixed coordinates
for what you found
and all travellers set out
from where they are.
Freedom is the only cry.
It exists, is the best we can say.

At Hand

Just slightly on from where you stand
is the answer to the question
you've been holding.
A little beyond
but not something you can reach
by walking further or pushing harder,
not something to see or hear by straining.

The step least taken is trusting
that the answer is in the air,
believing that help is here right now,
asking, knowing it is given,
pausing, so you might receive it,
allowing yourself to accept
the help at hand.

Here Now

Where else would you find it
besides where you are right now?
What good is peace, joy
or, heaven forbid, rest,
if it is always on the other side
of just one more thing?
It is not earned or worked towards,
you have always carried it with you.
Go on, check your pocket.
I left you a handful of quiet
to get things started.

On Asking

You were made for more than fitting in
and more than impressing others.
You didn't come to be chosen,
not for jobs, as friend or lover.
None of these are life goals
and we're sorry, we could not tell you sooner
that the well meant advice of others,
the mal-intent of the market
—this is how you get on in life
this is what you must do—
only sends you further from yourself.

We could not tell you sooner
that fitting in is not a goal,
but having a life that fits you is.
Impressing others is not important
but impressing upon yourself
that you need no blessing? That is.
That's important.
We could not tell you sooner,
you had to ask the question first,
had to wonder why trying
to fit and impress and be chosen
has left you nowhere.

But here you are now, asking,
so we tell you, and soon enough—
do not wait to be chosen,
choose for yourself,
choose your self,
and all is given.

Quiet

Only in quiet will you hear it,
the undercurrent, the base note
on which your song is built.

Only when still will you see it,
the flicker of light, the quick darting
movement of your otherself.

Only at ease will you feel it,
the subtle shifts, the slow turning,
something in you waking.

The Still Pond

Don't mistake silence for absence
or stillness for inaction.
Quieting the mind
takes effort like no other
and delaying the urge to move
takes practice.
Ignore the demands
to be other than you are.
The still pond hums with life.

When You Know

When you know who you are
there is no sense of time lost or life wasted.
Everything that came before,
all you did that was not this,
all you were that was not
who you are now, was vital,
all the times you were lost
helped you find your way.
There is no urgency,
no time to make up for,
you are not late.
When you know who you are
all is timeless.

Replenish

Ask nothing of me.
I'm tired
from the yeses
of yesterday
last week
last year
given not freely
but wrung out
drip by drip,
leaving me
dry.

I'm asking nothing
of myself today.
I'm resting.
This self
is refilling,
not one drop
will I spill
until
my own self
is well watered.

Freed

It was when the sun broke out
and danced through every raindrop,
turning gloom into something transcendent,
that I wondered
what if all that's hard
was washed away?

What if the light came down
and freed us all from regret, shame
and second-guessing?
What would there be
except sun glancing through water
and each of us dancing?

The Invitation

When you least expect it
you may find yourself back there again—
old thoughts, old hurts, alive once more.
Though what you thought was healed
seems open and sore again
you have done this work,
settled the past and healing begun.
You can return to it, or
step back from the edge,
feel your body say no,
press your palm to something new.
Come, meet your power.
Ask, what do I want instead?

Keep Something For Yourself

No matter the treasure bestowed on you
in the night, when you wake
keep something for yourself.

As you walk through your day
leaning into the lot that calls your name,
keep something for yourself.

And as you settle, giving thanks
for the grace you received this day,
always, keep something for yourself.

Wait

It's not that we're abandoned,
but that we demand delight at every turn.
We can only stay sated so long.
Even joy must be digested,
allowed to settle and feed the body.
Make space for hunger, boredom and fear
from which hollow
something new will emerge.
Wait for yearning,
wait for the willingness
to kindle a life,
to find and forage
for that which nourishes,
to walk and work for
that which does not need to be earned
after all, but lies waiting,
shadowed only by our lashes,
right before our desperate eyes.

Be Not Silent

Do not be silent.
Do not sideline yourself
to the imagined power of another.

Be silent only on your terms,
for your own listening,
for hearing what you long to speak,
and when your voice rises—
speak it.

When words inflate your chest,
your heart beating ahead of your mind
drumming its path for you,
it is time.

Even as your palms sweat
know this—
your body does not fear the speaking,
it is not afraid to be heard.

As you stand trembling,
as you hover on the lip of voice—
all your body fears
is that you might stay silent
yet again.

Another Way

Before the final leap
there are chances to practice,
moments to let go
and try another way,
tired as we are of the old
which promises more of the same
but never freedom.

We might call on help:
show me what I cannot see,
how else could I do this,
who might I be?
And then the part we often miss—
listen.

Change

Change can come like a slow dawn.
You shower, dress and make your way downstairs
to find the day has kicked off its boots,
let itself in and put the kettle on.
After all the sleepless nights,
there sits change,
waiting for you.

Clay

This clay pot has been hollowed out
one, two, three times already.
How much more can there be?
Still more, says Life.
There is still more freedom for you yet.

Terrain

When every hill looks like
the original mountain you had to climb
and every drop feels like
the cliff from which you first fell
remember that the terrain of a life
is deeper than the landscape of the day.
If you've scaled one
you can scale them all
and that fall, though frightening,
taught you to fly.

Mind

It was mind
that led you from the path,
and learning to direct it
can lead you home again.
Use the mind
to decide to go inward,
to determine to be still,
to reflect on the ways it deserts
but also obeys you.
The spade that dug the hole
can fill it again.

Joy

Do the joyous things,
the wasteful, indulgent, frivolous things.
Do them despite no time, no money, no point,
as if there was nothing to live up to
and no one to let down.
Do the joyous things,
forget lofty, worthwhile, respectable,
banish outcomes, forget waste.
Since when are you a factory?
Do all the if only I could things
all of the pointless, wonderful things,
The point after all is joy.
Do the joyous things.

Unafraid

Of course
it is hard to be still—
haven't we eyes that roam
and aren't there sounds to follow
and legs that itch to move
and don't we think
all that awaits us is
painful thoughts
and our hurting heart
which is true
but also, when still
we see the clouds moving,
we see the light slowly shifting,
we see a bird, twig in its beak,
fly deep into the tree, unafraid.

Awaken

From a great slumber you awaken.
Like the sleeping bear,
your hibernation was no mistake
and nor is your timing in rousing.
The stirring within
and signals with-out
align, a divine conjunction
inviting you now to rise.

As you slept
your stores were filled
and gifts bestowed,
leaving you ready in ways
you can't yet see, for challenges
to which you are now more than equal.
Trust me when I say
your spring is here.

Esteem

If it feels like the world
is too much for you,
you just haven't met it
on your own terms yet.

Under the dictate of others—
how to be in it,
what to do in it,
who you are in it,
what love is—
the world will always be
too much or not enough.

Right Action

Some people move
because they are adventurers,
others because it hurts to be still.

Some are still
because they're afraid,
for others, there lies adventure.

Who can say what is right for another?
The tree is rooted for a reason.
The cloud roams free for another.

The Line

When you find yourself
casting about,
throwing out lines
to test the water,
looking for what holds
or holds true in your life,
remember that the answer
always lies in the hand
that holds the line.

When Life Brings You to an Edge

Let yourself be sharpened,
let fall what is falling away.
See what remains.

Let yourself be sharpened
and question not
where the arrow now points.

As It Is

If you feel unfit for the world
your job may be to resist the calls
to get up and get going,

to become
even more still,
seek even more quiet,

to notice what others do not—
how beautiful this world is,
how complete
as it is.

This Way, Come

A curtain billows
letting in a draught of fresh air,
inviting a glimpse of what lies outside.

There is no singular view of anything,
no one way to get things done,
no right way to live

though at times your life might show itself
arriving in the dancing light,
landing with a soft stirring of air.

Rest

Acquaint yourself with quiet,
recognise the need in you for rest,
not to recover from that which is done
but to prepare for what is to come.
The still place is where everything collects.
Rest is the beginning, not the end.

Keep Going

You took it as far as it could go,
walked the road to its end
and just kept walking.
The road ran out, but
it turns out, you haven't.
On you've walked
through beginnings,
middles and ends,
and still you're here,
still you're walking.

Rearrange

This is not the fruitless kind,
the rearranging of deck chairs
as the ship goes down,
rather, the vital allowing
of the outside to match the in,
the inner life meeting the world anew.
When we pull a piece
from the bottom row
things may fall.
Or at least, lean heavily.
Or at least, let's hope so.
We may be a chain of links
and a story of parts,
but our whole is remade
with every small change.
Nothing is forever,
nothing is set in a way
that can't be altered.
Rearrange an old piece,
create one part anew,
rebirth again and again.

Pennies

Spend them on joy,
those pennies held tight in your fist.
Don't deposit them in worry
or give them to guilt.
Invest them in enchantment.
Enjoy the return.

While You Can

Don't wish it away
because of confusion,
hopelessness and pain,
it's over all too soon as it is.
Eat the ice cream while you can,
graze your knee from stumbling
while running too fast,
break the heart that loves so hard.
It mends. Love again.

Woven

We are knit together
in ways we cannot see,
the blanket of us
relying on each holding their place,
taking the space we've been given,
grounded, not swaying
centred, not leaning
whole, not with parts left out.

Loose

There's only so many loose ends you can leave
before you start encountering them again.
There they are, the untied,
the unexpressed, all you left open
from last time
still waiting for you.
They don't have to trip you up.
Pick them up, follow the trail
you left yourself on the last go round
or the round before that.

Hand over hand, feel as you go
events of all texture and ply.
Trace them back
to the one you first let fall.
Hold it, listen to its story.
Love the hand that dropped it,
love the trail it left,
the way it kept you safe,
the ways it got you here alive.
Find the first loss, that first undoing
then follow the loose end home.

Homeward

One day it's done, behind you
the past and all it meant
in the rear view mirror.
The mountainous climb,
the frightening descent,
the fog on that lonely road.
That part is over, the past in the past,
ahead clear and open
and you, heading home.

Pieces

This is a time of unearthing,
uncovering all that lies buried.
We can howl at the moon all we like
but her light reflects our sharp edges
only so we see them
glinting in the dark at our feet.
This is not meant to hurt us.
Each pointed moment
is a piece of our puzzle,
each shard of hurt
carefully brought to light
remakes us whole.
Let the moon light upon you,
let her show you where to look.

Imminent

What feels imminent is present,
what is latent is already alive.
Who you are becoming
is not ahead of you in time
nor separate in space
but with you right now
guiding your life.

The Stream

We can travel far from what sustains us.
We are explorers, are we not?
When lost it is natural to seek
higher ground, hoping to see new vistas
and leave the tangled undergrowth behind.

Always we can count on the water.
It takes quiet, and an ear tuned to hear it,
to catch the singing stream calling us closer,
inviting us back to where we began,
pointing, always, to the sea.

Resolution

Everything leans toward resolution.
Clouds part to reveal the sky,
the water runs to clear,
bare soil does not stay bare for long.
The arc of a life always bends
to take you home.

New

The world is brand new today, do you feel it?
Don't be fooled by your senses,
by what seems the same around you.
Every object is alive,
empty space is always dancing in new ways.
The world is born again today,
and so are you.

Trust the Tide

It's hard to believe
things are improving
when we start to feel worse,
as if walked on by life yet again.

But the mind is full of the past
as it starts to make peace
and the body is just releasing
what the heart let go.

Simply watch, and remember,
the incoming tide always goes out,
taking our footprints with it.

The Path

The path, once narrow, widens now.
The way that would appear
then recede from view
has been pressed open by a thousand feet.
The alternate route becomes the highway.

Vessel

As you feel the slowing,
the shrinking, the wrinkling
the ageing, feel yourself
disengaging from the
patterns, from waging
war with yourself,
when your body no longer
wants to scale the
mountains placed there
by others,
when it seems the body
has reached its peak,
you'll find a new one waiting,
a body of knowing and light
that needs no vehicle,
that shines
whatever the vessel,
vaster than you know,
stronger than you think,
more secure than ever.

Ever Learning

I am an apprentice
and hope always to be
often stumbling
ever learning
always in awe.

Beyond the Map

Even the map must go, then.
that brittle page in your pocket,
worn at the edges, softly creased
with markings faint and faded,
the map you've folded, unfolded
and folded again.

Though it led you from lost
to hopeful, even maps run out,
land streaming over the edges,
life waterfalling in every direction,
the map itself bowing
under the weight
of your desire
to just go.

So, go on. You know the way.
Drop all that is not yours,
even the map.

What I Want From Life

Whittled like a stick,
time and intention
narrowing what matters,
only one thing is left
with which I cannot argue—
let me do what I came here for.

Re-Entry

When life sends you stratospheric,
or you yourself leave it all
in search of what lies behind
the thin blue line of your imagination,
turn and look down upon
all that has loomed large
and overwhelming.

How big the world is.
How different each life
and how much the same.
See how there's no point comparing?
See how each life is its own?

When you return,
for return we must,
let all that is not you
burn upon re-entry.
Land soft and open
on the belly of the earth.

It's Not Too Late

It's not too late
to build rock walls with your bare hands,
to lay brick paths, weave a nest,
make sculpture for your garden.

There's still time to draw and paint,
to make real the pictures in your mind,
and birth the lands you visit
when you dream.

It's not too late
to go to wild places, alone,
and unafraid.
Stand on the cliff tops,
stare at the heaving sea,
drape yourself
like weed over its rocks.

You could still remember how to roar,
make your body strong,
feel like you belong in it.

It's not too late to write
all the things that whisper to you.
Press your ear to the chest of the earth
and hear its quiet breathing.
Trace a vein, listen for
that which has no name yet.
Name it.

You could change gear, go slowly.
Move through the world,
through each day at your own pace;
drop to the grass, follow the ant's path
through the forest if you choose.

Disregard the rules.
Drop them like a heavy coat.
Follow the call, sure as an ancient traveller
following stars as they sail the blind ocean.
Set out, sail free.
Navigate by the star that you are.

Home

On the day you finally meet yourself
like a weary traveller home,
you will know it
the way a child knows her mother's hand
as something felt,
remembered.
You will know it in your flesh,
in the softening of your gait,
in the moment that you, finally
slip off your dusty shoes
and allow yourself
to rest.

INDEX OF FIRST LINES

Acquaint yourself with quiet   70
A curtain billows   69
After a long time unmoored   31
After the freeze comes the thaw   17
Ask nothing of me   50
As you feel the slowing   85

Before the final leap there are chances to practice   56

Change can come like a slow dawn   57
Clear the rubble, sweep the soil   32
Come home though you don't know you're gone   15
Cradled in your palm you have kept the flame alive   41
Curl yourself around it   37

Do not be silent   55
Don't fear the fall-out   20
Don't mistake silence for absence   48
Don't placate the parts of you that want to scream
and cry   28
Don't wish it away   74
Do the joyous things   61

Each day splits into two, again and again   35
Even the map must go, then   87
Everything leans toward resolution   81

Frightening thoughts are roads of no return   42
From a great slumber you awaken   63

Grace comes the way a whale comes   33

Heal me then, but gently   27
How many lenses we look through   25

I am an apprentice   86
If it feels like the world is too much for you   64
If you feel unfit for the world   68
If you find yourself rattling the cage of your life 24
In the end the moment of change is imperceptible   19
It's hard to believe things are improving   83
It's not others that threaten your flame   38
It's not that I want to improve anything   23
It's not that we're abandoned   54
It's not too late   90
It was mind that led you from the path   60
It was when the sun broke out   51

Just slightly on from where you stand   44

Let yourself be sharpened   67

No matter the treasure bestowed on you   53

Of course it is hard to be still   62
One day it's done, behind you   77
Only in quiet will you hear it   47
On the day you finally meet yourself   92

Spend them on joy, those pennies   73
Some people move because they are adventurers   65
Sometimes we have to go back to go forward   16

That something you feel called to   39
The events of our life will sometimes channel our
attention   26
The flame of a candle always licks upward   40
The path, once narrow, widens now   84
There's only so many loose ends you can leave   76

The seagulls are circling 34
The world is brand new today, do you feel it? 82
This clay pot has been hollowed out 58
This is a time of unearthing 78
This is it 30
This is not the fruitless kind 72

Unhitch yourself from the wagon 29

We are knit together 75
We can travel far from what sustains us 80
We want the dam to break 18
What feels imminent is present 79
When every hill looks like the original mountain 59
When life sends you stratospheric 89
When the fire won't catch 36
When you find freedom 43
When you find yourself casting about 66
When you know who you are 49
When you least expect it 52
When you wake into the great loneliness 22
Where else would you find it 45
Whittled like a stick 88

You may come loose from the fabric of your life 21
You took it as far as it could go 71
You were made for more than fitting in 46

ACKNOWLEDGEMENTS

Thank you to the team that helped turn this collection of poems into the beautiful book you hold in your hands. Thank you to Sara Gaspar for yet another magnificent cover design. Thank you to Denika Mead and Sophie White for the typesetting and internal design, and to Sophie again for getting this beautiful book print ready. Thank you also to Julie Postance, whose help and guidance with my previous books is still felt in this one.

My deep thanks to Marion Rose Ph.D., whose vision of the world allowed me to see and sustain my own. Thank you for your unwavering faith in the goodness of human beings, and your trust in the unfolding of each person's life.

Thank you to all of my family. A special thank you to Hamish, the ever steady rock to my burbling, fanciful stream. And to my sister Bernadette who, across time and space, has held my hand through the hardest of times.

Finally, thank you to the unseen forces that send the energy of poems my way. It's my great privilege to bring them to life.

MARY WALKER was born in Aotearoa New Zealand to a Kiwi mother and Irish father. She lives with her husband and children in Te Awa Kairangi ki Uta Upper Hutt.

She is the author of the poetry collections *Lullaby for Mothers: motherhood in poems* (2019) and *The Land Will Hold You* (2022).

A Beautiful Beginning is her free poetry subscription. Subscribe to receive the weekly emails at her website.

www.marywalker.co.nz

Instagram @mary_walker_writer

Printed by Libri Plureos GmbH in Hamburg, Germany